Praise for **V**

"Finally! A book that gives you sound, practical advice on how to be successful on the job and in your career. This is a must read for job seekers, recent college graduates, and those looking to switch careers. It all starts with *Would you hire you?*"

-Therese Dickerson, Director of Recruiting, International Bridge

"Developing leaders who can help shape the 21st century is no easy task. However, this book provides excellent tips on how organizations and individuals can bring ownership and compassion to the work they do."

-Nimir Raval, Social Worker/Community Builder, City of Edmonton

"This is a fantastic book! Great advice on everything from handling difficult conversations to dealing with different personality types. It's full of real life examples which brings the book to life. An excellent follow up to *Canadian Workplace Culture*!"

-Debbie Mastel, Critical Talent Specialist, Devon Energy

"An informative read that is thorough yet practical. The real-world scenarios offer a profound vision of a respectful and empathetic workplace."

-Eric VandeVelde, Chair, Publications/Social Media, HRPA Ottawa

"A valuable go-to guide that will definitely assist you in achieving greater job satisfaction and security. Matt's clear, concise, and hands-on ideas can be quickly utilized to help you navigate today's changing world of work."

-Ron Volk, Coordinator of Employment Services, CCIS

Would You Hire You?

Great to meet you Annette!

Matt

Would You Hire You?

Matt Adolphe

IGUANA

Copyright © 2015 Matt Adolphe
Published by Iguana Books
720 Bathurst Street, Suite 303
Toronto, Ontario, Canada
M5V 2R4

Publisher: Greg Ioannou
Editor: Veronica Adolphe
Front cover design: Daniella Postavsky
Book layout design: Kathryn Willms

Library and Archives Canada Cataloguing in Publication

Adolphe, Matt, author
    Would you hire you? / Matt Adolphe.

Includes bibliographical references and index.

Issued in print and electronic formats.

ISBN 978-1-77180-156-0 (paperback).--ISBN 978-1-77180-157-7 (epub).--ISBN 978-1-77180-158-4 (kindle)

    1. Organizational behavior--Canada. 2. Work environment--Canada. 3. Language in the workplace--Canada. I. Title.

HD58.7.A36 2015   302.3'5   C2015-907039-2
                                    C2015-907040-6

This is an original print edition of *Would You Hire You?*

For Harry

Also by the author

Canadian Workplace Culture:
Mastering the Unspoken Rules

Table of Contents

Acknowledgements

First and foremost, acknowledgement must go to my wife, Veronica, who continues to be such a major contributor. She is wonderful and has been incredibly helpful throughout the whole writing process. She is a remarkable editor and I am deeply indebted to her for all her encouragement and support. Likewise, since a great part of the writing process takes place at home, our children, Joseph, Edward, and Gabriella, are continually demonstrating how wonderfully supportive and understanding they can be. They are small but they have very big hearts.

Also, appreciation goes out to all my friends, colleagues, and students, who encouraged me to continue writing, and to everyone who participated in the talks, presentations, and workshops over the last few years. The world is truly a beautiful place with all of you in it.

Matt Adolphe
Calgary
December 2015

Preface

This book represents a natural follow-up project to *Canadian Workplace Culture: Mastering the Unspoken Rules*. In the past few years, through various talks and workshops, many people have shared their reactions to that book. What struck me from those reactions was a noticeable and overwhelming desire to learn more about how to have job security and satisfaction. So *Would You Hire You?* strives to introduce those skills that individuals need to be highly successful in their careers.

Things are happening fast in the world of work, especially with the emergence of our newest generation—the first technologically native generation, "Generation Z," in the workplace. Like Gen Y before it, Gen Z presents another game changer for the rest of the generations. Their fast and highly entrepreneurial mindsets offer exciting opportunities for all industries. And if you thought change was fast before, you have not seen anything yet. And this is only one part of the reality that we face every day as we aim for success along our chosen career paths.

Therefore, in response to the uncertainty of our future, this book aims to help everyone put that uncertainty into perspective. In the end, the only way we can keep on top of the changing world of work is to keep ahead of those changes.

Introduction

This book proposes 10 tips to help you excel in your job in this changing world of work. If you follow these tips, not only do you become an essential employee, but you also make work a better place for those around you. Let's call it a win-win situation.

We often hear people say, "I have worked for that company for fourteen years and they just laid me off." or "I have worked here longer than that person. Why am I being laid off first?"

We also note that working at the same job for 25 years and collecting a pension afterwards is no longer common in any industry these days. Contracts are for one to two years only; sometimes longer, but still nothing is guaranteed for the long run.

In any event, the key to getting ahead in your career and avoiding layoffs altogether is in your hands. You have to realize that with the advance of technology, everything changes much faster. Those with technical expertise and flexibility are favoured and depended on more. The key words here are *depended on*. Because when you are depended on, you have power at your job.

So you need to ask yourself: *Do I have power at my job?*

If your answer is, *No, anyone else can do my job*, you need to think deeply about what your career path is. Where do you want to go? What do you want to accomplish? Where do you want to be in five years?

We cannot just clock in and clock out, and do the same thing every day. The world is globally in tune with diversity, understanding, and technology. You need to be a citizen of the world to bring value to your organization.

Your world of work needs you to be sensitive and flexible to a multitude of things. You have to be flexible in job assignments. You have to learn and embrace new ideas. You have to possess superb communication and interpersonal skills. You have to be adaptable and diverse. These are areas that give you power in your job. Mastering skills in these areas makes you indispensable and puts you in control of your career path.

Ultimately, you need to be conscious of your impact at work and on others. You work in a results-powered world but you are still very much judged on how you treat others during the process of your work. In other words, completing tasks and meeting deadlines is essential, but that is not what defines who you are. Day after day, you get your work done and do what is required of you; you meet your sales quota, or you complete a project before the deadline, but does that make you a valuable employee? Does that build your reputation and win the respect of your colleagues? Does that help you keep your job or get ahead?

Allow me to tell you a little story to emphasize what I meant about how you are remembered and respected by the way you treat people during the process of your work.

What comes to your mind when you think of Thomas Edison?

You probably remember him as an inventor and as the person who brought us the light bulb. However, he gave us so much more.

Edison worked with a team of scientists and engineers to come up with the right combination of elements for a long, self-sustaining, electrically charged light bulb. They worked tirelessly and tried over 1500 variations before coming up with a solution.

Back in those days, you can imagine that the air in the lab was probably pretty hot and stuffy. Undoubtedly, their work area was dimly lit and full of commotion. Add to that, the team was under a lot of pressure; and tensions were high. Surely, it was just a matter of time before the breakthrough.

And all the while, watching with total amazement and awe was a young boy whose job was to keep the lab clean. Can you imagine the wonder and amazement in the boy's eyes as he watched the team work feverishly to change the world?

On one particular day, after the team worked almost 24 hours straight without sleep, something amazing happened. They felt they had achieved the right combination and a bulb was presented to Edison for testing.

However, Edison gave the bulb to the boy to place in the testing device. (You can be sure there were all kinds of grumblings from the tired and overworked team.)

Unfortunately, the boy, overwhelmed with emotions and the overall weight of the task, dropped the bulb. It smashed on the floor. (You can just imagine the reaction of the team of scientists and engineers.)

Anyway, hours later, the team assembled another bulb. However, when the scientists were ready to test the bulb, Edison called the boy over to place the bulb in the device.

Edison left us with a very valuable lesson—when you focus only on end results, you lose touch with humanity in the process. And when humanity is lost, goals lose meaning. Then, all is lost.

The reality is people create products and meet deadlines every day, but those we remember and admire most take time to make sure people are respected during the process of their work. They are our leaders and our champions. So let's learn from them and apply that humanity and concern for others in our work.

Throughout this book, we focus on skills you need to work with others. And by building this foundation of trust and understanding with those around you, you become invaluable to your organization. Also, this puts you in control of your career path and helps you navigate through the uneasy waters of constant organizational change.

1

Realize Customer Service Starts with You

We have all heard the phrase, "The customer is always right." And we all know that a business is successful only when its customers are satisfied. The same is true for employees (who are also customers of their business). So, your job is successful only when your customers, both internal and external, are satisfied.

You must understand the role of customers. Every one serves someone. Take time to understand who your customers are. (If it is not so apparent because you work in a massive company, then think about who your stakeholders are.) Who is impacted by your work and by how well you do it? And once you analyze who you serve, look to your colleagues and make sure you are giving them the same service as well.

Yes, that's right! Think about your colleagues as your customers. They are your internal customers and they deserve to be treated with the same care and respect as your external customers.

Here are some simple customer service tips you can apply to your everyday interaction with colleagues:

Give others your undivided attention. When people talk to you, make them the centre of your universe. Get off your cell phone or your computer, turn to them, and listen attentively. Don't look over your colleague's shoulder or answer a call too quickly. If someone else comes up to you when you are talking to your colleague, let the new person know politely that you were talking to that person first. A customer deserves this respect and so does your colleague.

Be polite. You know how important it is to be polite to customers. Your customers don't care what kind of mood you are in or how tired you are; they just want the service they expect. Also, when customers phone or send you an email, you respond courteously. Do the same for your colleagues as well.

Be ethical and principled. You do this for your customers, why not your colleagues? You try hard to see your customers' perspective, so do the same for your colleagues.

Be diplomatic. With your customers, you are solution-focused. Be the same with your colleagues as well. Don't take issues personally. Learn to respond rather than react.

Represent your organization's values. Apply your organization's values when working with your external customers and various stakeholders, as well as with your colleagues.

And nothing demonstrates your excellent customer service more than "the moment of truth," which is the moment you go that extra mile for your customers. Apply that in your everyday interactions with your colleagues as well. Go that extra mile!

For example, when you notice a messy washroom counter at work, instead of saying this is not your problem and leaving the mess for the maintenance department, how about you just clean that counter? You help the maintenance department look good and you show that the workplace belongs to everyone. Take that extra step!

I remember driving to work in January 2015 when I heard on the news that Target was closing all its stores in Canada. Over 17 000 employees were going to be laid off. The news was shocking and upsetting for many people, especially for the employees who were not given any prior notice. Can you imagine learning your organization's closing down at the same time the rest of the country does? Can you imagine going to work after hearing that news?

And as Target moved to liquidate its final stock to pay back its creditors, its sales were massive. The weeks leading up to its closing were its busiest and most chaotic. So not only were the staff soon to be unemployed, they were required to provide their best customer service as well. In addition to that, the prices were not as low as customers expected, so customer complaints were at an all-time high.

In the face of all this, many employees simply quit and walked off the job. *Why would I put myself through that?* they thought. And that was an understandable reaction. We might all do the same.

But there were those who stayed, working harder than ever because the stores were short-staffed. They put on their best face for their customers and their colleagues. And they offered support and encouragement to each other.

Now those are incredible employees! By merely staying on the job, with that attitude, they have set themselves up for success for the rest of their lives.

Just imagine, who would you hire? If you had to choose between two former Target employees? Would you choose the one who walked away (again an understandable response), or the one who chose to stay and offer customer and collegial support?

Those employees who stayed were demonstrating what the authors of *Fundamentals of Organizational Behaviour* describe as "organizational citizenship behaviour." This term refers to those who go beyond the requirements of their job description. In short, they embody the moment of truth. And these are the people highly sought after by organizations.

The fact is, your relationship with your external customers and your internal customers has to be consistent. Just look at the following ten things external customers have in common with internal customers:

1. They know a business is only as good as how it treats its customers.
2. They look for value and respect.
3. They want to know what is in it for them.
4. They have families that are affected by your relationship with them.
5. They talk to their friends about the experience they have with you.
6. They want to be treated ethically and fairly or they will quit and walk away.

7. They advertise and sell your products if they believe in you.
8. They have pride in their relationship with you; they respect you if you respect them.
9. They want to do business with you, or they wouldn't be there.
10. They are loyal to you if they are treated well.

But to be effective at maintaining a strong customer service attitude, you have to know where your mind is emotionally. And that is why it is important to evaluate where your needs are, because the two are very much connected.

By knowing your needs, you can chart a path for yourself to self-actualization. As Abraham Maslow, architect of the hierarchy of needs theory, explains, "This tendency might be phrased as the desire to become more and more what one is, to become everything that one is capable of becoming."

To get there, you need to fulfill a certain level of esteem needs; for example, promotion and respect from your peers. To get those, you need friendships and support from your team – the love needs. And those tie into first having a stable job with reasonable benefits – the safety needs. And because with a steady job and benefits, you are able to take care of your basic needs, such as food and shelter – the physiological needs.

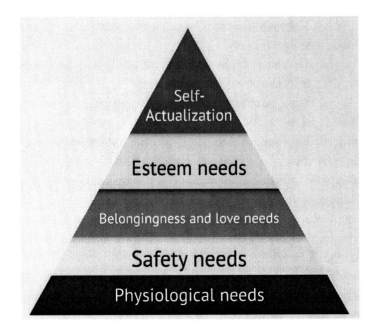

Maslow emphasizes that we often have percentages of each need fulfilled. And those percentages can change from time to time depending on where we are at in our career or personal life.

The point is there is not a lot of job security in the market these days, but you can't let yourself get bogged down with safety and physiological needs. And you can't afford to wait around to be rescued by others. If you are trapped there, you cannot be productive. If you are concerned only about job security, you can't focus on anything else but that worry. How can you provide solid customer service for anyone then? The real heroes are those who provide their excellent customer service in spite of the uncertainty of their future career.

You have to elevate yourself to esteem and self-actualization. When you provide excellent customer service, you inspire faith in your organization. And your reputation attracts like-mind individuals to work in your organization. Your attitude will inspire your colleagues to go that extra mile as well. And that's the true meaning of customer service. It all starts with you!

Now you understand the importance of providing that excellent customer service (to both your external and internal customers), so what's next? You need to *be visible and network*.

2

Be Visible and Network

The world of work has changed. Generally speaking, less than half of today's workforce enjoys a job with long-term security and benefits. Many people are even working several jobs or contracts. And even those with seemingly steady nine-to-five jobs are still at the mercy of year-to-year contracts. In other words, the world of work is uncertain—the tide could turn quite suddenly at any moment. And in an ocean of tumult, in order to be rescued you need to be visible.

Recently I met an individual who had received an extensive medical science background in another country. He got a job at a large medical research lab after immigrating to Canada. After eight years of work, his project's funding was cut and he was out of a job.

Does this story sound familiar? The job he did well every day was suddenly gone. Now what?

Why wouldn't the research lab give him more work, perhaps in another area? The lab is a big place, there must be some other work it could offer him. Or why wouldn't someone there help him find another job in another lab? Eight years is a long time, and with the great work he did, day in and day out, where was his support now?

This individual was invisible. He didn't build those connections that are necessary for support in uncertain times. So when the funding was gone, he too was gone.

Sadly, like many people transitioning into today's workforce, he was operating under his past assumption: if you work hard at the technical job you are paid to do, your career will be taken care of. Unfortunately, this is no longer the case.

In today's world of work, you need to be visible. You need to create a good reputation of being diligent, creative, and flexible and, most of all, of having great interpersonal communication skills. When you are visible, people depend on you, because they see value in you. And when you are valuable, you are irreplaceable.

You need to constantly build networks inside and outside your work. You can't afford to put all your eggs in one basket. You can like the basket you are in, enjoy the work you do, but you can't risk being too comfortable at your job, or you become unprepared for major market or economic shifts.

Be visible, talk to people, and make connections. This starts within your own organization. Get yourself known by as many colleagues as you can. Your name should be somewhat familiar to everyone. You need colleagues to know your name and know you exist. (And if you find that people do know you but their opinion of you is not great, don't despair—this is not a bad thing! By knowing how you are perceived by others, you can reflect and improve that image.)

Get known by your manager and be available if he needs your help—be indispensable. Also, bring him solutions, not problems.

Apart from being known among your colleagues, network as much as you can outside your organization. Join LinkedIn and get connected with other professionals in your group. You need to have an online presence these days. It is considered suspicious if you don't. You may appear anti-social, or simply technologically illiterate.

You need to stay current with changes in your field and join in-person and virtual groups like seminars and events.

The following story helps demonstrate how important it is to join events.

While participating in a local charity event for the Animal Rescue Foundation, a woman met another participant with whom she had a conversation. At the end of the day, the person said to her, "You know, it was so nice talking to you, do you mind me asking what you do?"

She responded, "Well, I'm an administrative assistant, but I'm not working right now."

The person then said, "I work in the executive office for a major energy provider. Why don't you come by on Monday and we can talk? I actually have an opening for an admin position that I think you would be perfect for."

On Monday, she went to that company and was hired.

The fact is, leaders in organizations often attend these kinds of events. It is their way to give back to the community. You simply never know who you are going to meet. There are so many opportunities for you to meet people. Take advantage of every opportunity.

Also, take advantage of every professional development opportunity. Take courses offered by your organization. By taking courses to upgrade your skills, you can inspire others to have more confidence in you.

You need to be current. It is crucial in such quickly changing times that you are up-to-date on all issues and trends in your field. Do you have the right training? Do you update your skill set, keeping it sharp? The people around you are the first to notice that you are not keeping up.

Let me tell you another little story to reinforce this point.

I taught an evening English conversation class at a local college several years ago. In that class were newcomers in various stages of their careers. I was surprised that a chief financial officer of a large company was in the class. She was already very high up, and probably well paid. Her first language was Spanish, and although her English was not totally fluent, I was able to understand her clearly. She explained that she had lived in Canada for a long time and had worked at her organization for a while, but her English had not really improved and colleagues were losing confidence in her. She exclaimed, "If it's so apparent to others that I am not improving my own skills, how can I demand that of others?"

In actuality, several wonderful things happen when you take these courses. First of all, these courses increase your skills. Second, your increased skills boost the confidence others have in you. Third, you meet people and your network grows. And last, you stay current with the changes in your field. In the end, it all looks great on a résumé too!

People have said to me, "When a company downsizes, layoffs are a reality. It doesn't matter what I do if my company lays people off, all of this is worthless then."

Yes, this is a reality we all face, especially with today's new technological and shifting world markets. At times, companies have to, for whatever reason, make staff cuts. While in some cases there is only one wave of layoffs—the organization shuts down, like Target Canada. However, in most cases, layoffs happen in stages.

A friend of mine who works in human resources in the energy industry recently told me that he was quietly working on the first wave of layoffs. He said he was quietly going through all the performance reviews and was first cutting those who were poor communicators and "who nobody would really miss."

In the first stage, organizations cut the fat—the low producers. The ones who bring no real value to their position. The ones who are expendable and are not depended on. Many in this category are those who never really fit in to begin with.

My friend said that if they have to make even further cuts, they then turn to those who don't have the stamina or will to take on more work in a reduced staff environment— the friendly, hard-working but inflexible types. They are the people who just do the minimum. They don't volunteer for extra hours or responsibilities. They only take courses if they are required to. They are not real catalysts for change. So, they are gone.

And if there is a third wave, those are the employees organizations least want to cut. They are valuable, well trained and essential. They are those who demonstrate "organizational citizenship behaviour." Their organization wants them, but there are simply no new contracts. And this is the moment of true heartbreak for their organization. They have no choice but to let their most prized and appreciated employees go.

If you are in that third wave of layoffs, there are a lot of good things you can leverage. In other words, if you have a good reputation, you have an advantage of getting more support. For example, even though it may not be company policy to write letters of recommendations for employees, you might find rules bent a bit for you. Perhaps your manager can write a private letter for you. And your manager would because she knows this recommendation will not come back to haunt her. (Reference letters are discouraged or even forbidden by most organizations because organizations could be sued for "negligent misrepresentation" if their recommended employees turn out to be completely incompetent at their new jobs. Even though, according to employment lawyer, Elizabeth Reid, "It's not likely, but why take the risk?")

In addition, your work portfolio is essential. That's right. If you haven't been keeping up your portfolio already, it is best you get started.

Keep every email and written comment about your work. Get people to endorse you on LinkedIn. You need to be able to display your track record.

Performance reviews are also very important—they are more important than reference letters. Of course I am assuming you work hard and your reviews are all great, although I did hear that a single mishap that occurs even a week or two before your performance review can sometimes overshadow your whole year's good performance. Nevertheless, keep good records, and be consistent with your good work.

Anyway, the point here is keep those positive comments and reviews of your work all in portfolio — *keep everything!*

You have to make an effort to build your own career path. You do not want to be in that first wave of layoffs, nor do you want to keep making lateral moves. By being visible and current, and by taking the time to network, you demonstrate your "organizational citizenship behaviour." You then move upward, not side to side. And ultimately, how you build your reputation is essential. To make it to the top, you have to be known for putting people first in all you do. You can't do that if you think only about yourself. So, let's now explore the need for you to stop talking and start listening; *don't be a conversational narcissist*!

3
Don't Be a Conversational Narcissist

In the textbook, *Interpersonal Communication: Relating to Others,* the authors explain, "During conversations with a self-absorbed communicator, it is difficult sustaining communication about anything else except the self-absorbed partner's ideas, experiences, and stories."

Does this remind you of anyone you know? A conversational narcissist is a person who just does not stop talking about herself. Every conversation is all about her. You feel that your job is to simply stand there and listen.

Nobody likes living or working with these kinds of individuals, unless of course they are similar in nature. This type of individual does not care about anyone but himself. In fact, he is so self-absorbed — as the authors put it — he does not even notice the impact he has on others. He does not see that others are trying to avoid him. He does not see others' frustration when listening to him. He does not notice how others try to change the topic or end the conversation. He does not care if others are bored. He actually believes others are as interested in him as he is in himself. This is because he has no empathy for others.

It is sad, but there are many conversational narcissists out there. And in most cases, depending on how they were raised, they may not even notice they are acting that way. Self-absorbed communication is probably just the norm among their early life influencers.

According to management guru Peter Drucker, some individuals may be the type who "learn by hearing themselves talk." They have a style that they need people to "talk at," rather than "talk to" so they can see a situation more clearly.

Whatever the case may be, the following identifies various types of conversational narcissists:

1.   Those who ask you about something, just so you can ask them about the same thing

Your friend asks about your work, just so you ask about hers and she can talk all about her work. She asks about your kids, just so you ask about hers and she can talk all about her kids. And in the end, it doesn't matter if you talk about your work or your kids, all she wants is for you to ask about hers so she can talk about her business.

2.   Those who brag subtly (between the lines)

Your dentist talks about how he had to fix his son's teeth after a sport-related injury. He goes on to mention his son's hockey. And then it comes out, "My son plays at a very high intensity level of hockey." All of this is completely brought up without you even asking. Of course with all that stuff in your mouth, how can you?

3.   Those who complain, but are actually bragging

Your neighbour talks about how much work he does for his child, how many toys he buys, how many sporting activities he arranges, how many trips he takes so his child sees the world, how many birthday parties he plans, how many playdates he organizes—Oh, he is so tired—He complains, but is he actually just bragging about how good of a parent he is?

4.   Those who use Facebook for narcissistic reasons

Take for example, Jade Ruthven's shocking story of how a group of her colleagues wrote her an anonymous letter explaining their displeasure of her use of Facebook:

> Jade,
>
> I have got together with a few of the girls and we are all SO OVER your running commentary of your life and every single thing Addy does. Look we all have kids that we are besotted with—guess what—every parent thinks their kid is the best ever. But we don't ram it down everyone else's neck!!! She wears a new outfit—well take a photo and send it PRIVATELY to the person who gave it to her—not to everyone!!! She crawls off the mat—we DON'T care!!!!! She's 6 months old—BIG DEAL!!!! Stop and think—if every mother posted all the crap about their kid—I'm sure you'd get over it pretty quickly.

According to Gwendolyln Seidman's article, "Is Facebook Really Turning Us into Narcissists?" she explains that several studies show, "that a lot of what is seen on social media may be narcissistic. Several studies have shown that frequent Facebook users are likely to be more narcissistic. Narcissists also tend to post more self-promoting content."

Why did Jade get this reaction from her colleagues? What was so self-promoting about what Jade did?

Could it be that Jade's colleagues were aware of the research and thought she was showing off her perfect child? Could it be that this was what Jade's colleagues used their Facebook for, so they assumed she did the same? Perhaps narcissists just always assume other people are competing with them.

Perhaps in the end, people naturally despise what they themselves are. For example, people who hate conversation interrupters often interrupt conversations themselves. Likewise, people who hate cheapness in others are often cheap themselves. Carl Jung, a well-known psychiatrist and psychotherapist, referred to this as "shadow projection," when "other people observe their own unconscious tendencies in other people."

Whatever the case may be, the point here is important: do you know how people perceive you, either face-to-face or through your use of social media? Are you overly focused on yourself?

5.   Those who join fad ventures and always talk about it

Your sister, who is now very enthusiastic about a new trend—a diet plan—revolves her every conversation around that diet plan. Every day, she eats something new and talks about how healthy that is. She examines your lunch and talks about how she used to eat like that and how she makes changes. Her new fascination or hobby is all she is interested in talking about. And when the novelty of that fad passes, she latches onto another, and the cycle continues.

6.   Those who promote themselves through their advice

Your uncle always phrases his advice like, "Well, what I do is…" And often you do not even ask for his advice, he just gives it to you. He talks at great lengths about how his methods work for him and the people he has advised. He always has advice, and his advice has always worked for others.

7.   Those who continuously have the need to top stories (story toppers)

You talk about an amazing weekend you had and your cousin enters the conversation with a better weekend story. You say you went skiing at a well-known resort near the city, your cousin says she went heli-skiing on glaciers. You saw a funny YouTube video and she saw a funnier one. It goes on and on and she seems in need to be always one step ahead of everyone else in the conversation.

8.   Those who see nothing but a negative world view and assume everyone shares their same pessimism about life

You try to be positive about a change in the office, your colleague shuts you down with, "It won't work." or "We tried that before." You say something to the contrary, he gives you another negative point. Whatever positive response you have, he launches into more evidence of why his pessimistic picture is the only way you can look at the situation. He just dominates the conversation with negativity.

9. Those who actually believe people enjoy them for their witty stories and adventures—in which they always look better than anyone else (the entertainers)

Your aunt who thinks she is so appreciated for her sense of wit and charm feels you should just listen and be entertained by her stories. She talks about how she reacts to unreasonable people. She is the central character, the protagonist, the morally well-balanced individual coming to terms with an unreasonable and faulty world. She revels in describing the follies, stupidities, and misfortunes of others. She recants embarrassing stories of others, not of herself.

A great example that portrays this group of individuals is Jerry Seinfeld. In the show *Seinfeld*, Seinfeld himself somehow always looks better than his friends. Every other character in the series made fools of themselves, by being odd and unreasonable on a regular basis, whereas Jerry was more involved in situations dealing with people who were odd and unreasonable.

What would you expect from a program named for its main—*real life*—character? There is only one Seinfeld, and you are not he.

10. Those who constantly talk topics to death no one else cares about

Your brother-in-law who watches politics closely always talks about politics. He doesn't seem to care if you are interested or not. Your sister-in-law always talks about this

TV show that you don't even watch. Your friend, who can't get the idea out of his head that the book is better than the movie, won't stop talking about the book when you talk about the movie. Whatever the topic, they don't stop to think if others are at all interested in what they have to say. They get fixated on a topic, which has no relevance or interest to anyone listening.

11. Those who think professional networking is all about what *you* do for *them*

Have you ever been approached through LinkedIn or through other referrals or networking events, and you agree to meet somebody, only to find that person dominate the discussion about himself?

If you are going to be a successful networker, bring some value to other people. Ask what you can do for them. Networking has a lot to do with negotiation, and both sides should benefit from it. If the conversation is all about you, then your networking style does more harm than good for you.

In short, conversational narcissists put themselves before others. They see themselves as the smart ones, the centre of the universe, and everyone else revolves around them like the planets around the sun. And they see your job as the listener is to know your place in the conversation and respond in such a way that maintains them in the central role.

We find conversational narcissists everywhere. They could be our colleagues, our friends, our family members... They could be us! They may not be conscious of what they are doing, so the idea here is to give these individuals notice that monopolizing conversations, or putting too much out there on social media does not give them more power at work. It diminishes their power. Because even though people listen to them, it does not mean what they say is appreciated.

Power comes from showing others you are not more important than they are. You want to display a conversational style that is empathetic and caring. This is how you show respect for others, in return for their respect. In short, listen to others. Be that listener—put others first in your conversations.

Now that you are respected for being a strong listener, instead of a talker, you can *be skilled at difficult conversations.*

4

Be Skilled at Difficult Conversations

Difficult conversations are, by definition, difficult. They are common in the workplace. They can be conversations about complaints or performance issues. They can be conversations about someone's behaviour, appearance, or hygiene. They can be conversations about unreasonable demands, harassment, or bullying.

I heard from someone that for a long time she thought she was disliked by her colleagues because they avoided sitting next to her at lunch. It turned out that it was only because her perfume was too strong. By avoiding having that conversation with her, her colleagues actually avoided her altogether. She misunderstood and thought no one liked her.

How many of us have avoided these kinds of conversations? It is difficult to tell our colleagues things like this because they seem so personal.

Perhaps instead of avoiding difficult conversations, we should learn to be skilled at them, so that we can help each other to fit in.

Difficult conversations are about dealing with the issue while not trying to hurt a person's feelings. So let's analyze some strategies to help you tackle these conversations.

First and foremost, you need to have a reputation of being courteous (be a listener, not a talker). If you are always positive and polite, people understand you are not attacking them, you are simply trying to help them.

In *Managing Oneself*, Peter Drucker comments, "Manners—simple things like saying 'please' and 'thank you' and knowing a person's name or asking after her family—enable two people to work together whether they like it or not."

Drucker continues, "Bright people, especially bright young people, often do not understand this. If analysis shows that someone's brilliant work fails again and again as soon as cooperation from others is required, it probably indicates a lack of courtesy—that is, a lack of manners."

So the point here is simple: the first step to difficult conversations is building your reputation as a well-mannered colleague. That way, people are more accepting of your perspective. So once you have established a reputation as a well-mannered individual (a listener, not a talker) then difficult conversations should be fairly reasonable to deal with. People will generally want to solve problems with you.

And when the time comes for that difficult conversation, here are some helpful strategies:

1. Find the right time and place for it. (Remember: difficult conversations should be private.)
2. Buffer the conversation with some small talk. (Start with something simple and brief like, "Are you pretty busy or do you have time to talk?" or "How has your week been?")

3. Indicate your wish to discuss a particular issue by considering how it affects both of you. (Approach the issue, and don't make it personal).
4. Be open to hearing the other person's perspective without judging him. (Remember: you want to help.)
5. Have an assertive but professional and courteous tone. (Show you take the matter seriously.)
6. Avoid making "you" statements. Focus on "I" statements instead. You can say, "I feel…" or "I have noticed…" or "I have been thinking about something and I would like to talk to you about." (It is not personal.)
7. Slow down your tone and make it sound neutral. (Show that you care about the other person.)
8. Try to mimic the body language of the other person. (This shows empathy.)
9. Come up with some commitments that help you both move forward in a positive way. (Remember: You are a team.)
10. Close with a friendly air to the conversation. (End how you began—with a little small talk.)

Also, the art of having difficult conversations is knowing when and how to have them. You need to weigh the severity of the issue before you react. Having the confidence to have difficult conversations is important, but keep in mind that you do not always have to be the one to have them.

If you see your colleagues having a difficult conversation that does not affect you directly, don't interfere. It's tough to see your colleagues in that position, but it is really up to them to have that difficult conversation.

Perhaps some difficult conversations need to happen between an employee and a manager, and hopefully they both have the tact and skill to have that conversation. In other words, if you notice a behavioural problem, like an employee who is frequently late, you should leave that conversation for the manager and that employee. That is a managerial conversation. You don't want to behave like you are the manager. That is not a good reputation to have either. Therefore, you don't always need to get involved. And you don't want to be going to the manager all the time to tell her that she needs to have those conversations with other employees, or you may be perceived as something other than a concerned employee.

In other cases, some people may persuade you to help them with their difficult conversations. They may say, "Can you talk to him?" "You are so much better at doing that than I am." The truth is, others need to take responsibility for their work-related woes. If your colleagues ask you to step in on their behalf, sorry to say, but you have to review your priorities. You may help them by giving some advice on what they should do, but you have to make it clear that you cannot speak up for them. There are just certain times you need to avoid difficult conversations especially if those issues do not affect you directly. If you are always going out of your way to have difficult conversations with everyone, even those who you do not even work closely with, you will be perceived as a busybody.

Being skilled at difficult conversations is fine for most small, work-related issues; however, if you are being harassed or bullied, you need to escalate this issue to human resources. You have the right to feel safe and protected at work. Organizations are set up to help you overcome these situations. If someone is making improper advances or simply harassing you, seek out professional help from within your organization to help you with these bullies.

Standing up to bullies is not always easy (ask any teenager going through that at school). In the workplace, the same situation often happens. These people are difficult to deal with. Some bullies are clever: they know their boundaries and how far they can push without crossing the line where their position is in jeopardy. This is a kind of sociopathic behaviour.

The author of *The Sociopath Next Door*, Dr. Martha Stout, indicates one out of 25 Americans is a sociopath. This is a shocking figure, I know. You may very well be working with one of them. And why is it important to identify them? So you know how to deal with their self-centred, and manipulative personalities. Difficult conversations take on a new dimension with these individuals.

Stout's research describes that you can identify a sociopath in your workplace by a few certain traits. First, they are friendly, but are looking to dominate conversations. They probably rank among your conversational narcissists. Second, they believe that everything belongs to them. If there is anything they want, they go after it at whatever cost. Third, and it should come as no surprise, they simply lack any ability to empathize with others. They simply do not care what you think of them. And they certainly do not care if you are hurt by their behaviour. Fourth, to get what they want, they will not hesitate to lie. And according to Stout, "The best clue is, of all things, the pity play."

Generally, they are simply deceitful and calculating. In other words, they manipulate you by making you feel sorry for them. They continue with their abusive behaviours and cry saying they can't help themselves. They feed on your natural human tendency to feel for another human being. Stout concludes by saying, "Sociopaths have no regard whatsoever for the social contract, but they do know how to use it to their advantage."

When you encounter these types of individuals, you need a more assertive approach. You do not have to spend so much time buffering with small talk. In fact, the sooner you broach the topic and focus on the issue at hand, the better. Don't give them time to make you feel sorry for them. And if they are the type that are abusive, do not hesitate to escalate the situation to a higher authority in your organization.

In the end, we learn these skills because we do/should naturally care about people, just as organizations care about their customers. Now that you have confidence with difficult conversations, let's tackle the next hurdle in your world of work. Let's talk business. Let's *learn to negotiate*!

5

Learn to Negotiate

I feel the need to include this chapter after a recently taught negotiation course. My participants consisted mainly of senior salespersons. I doubted their need for such a course, but they expressed that junior salespersons were beating them at sales. So they needed to find out what the young people were learning. I then concluded that perhaps it's time we all updated our negotiating skills.

Often we find negotiation difficult. However, little do we realize that we negotiate every day; for example, we negotiate through traffic or public transportation to and from work, we jostle for space in elevators, we negotiate with our kids to eat their vegetables. In the end, we are in a constant state of negotiation. The question is: why is it so nerve-wracking when we deal with formal negotiations? And how can we better face these negotiations we deal with all the time?

Whether you have to negotiate during job interviews, contract discussions, or when working with colleagues, you can use the following strategies to improve your negotiation skills.

First, you need to prepare for the situation. Analyze your audience and develop a strategy that appeals to them. Also, be keenly aware of the hidden audience.

Who may be the real one pulling the strings or exerting pressure on your intended audience? By identifying all the players and their interests before planning your negotiation, you are setting the foundation for a successful negotiation. Ultimately, what we look for is a win-win situation. The outcome of a negotiation must be realistic and acceptable to both parties.

Authors of *Getting to Yes: Negotiating Agreement Without Giving In*, emphasize the importance of having a BATNA—Best Alternative to a Negotiated Agreement. There are times you need an alternative plan. For example, if you are negotiating for more pay, it would be helpful to let the other party know that you have been approached by another company.

When encountering negotiations, you may want to spend some time planning your BATNA. With a strong BATNA, you are more prepared for a negotiation. For example, if you are unhappy with your current job and you want to quit, look for another job first. It is always easier to find a job when you have one. In other words, create a BATNA before you make any move. And if it is a strong one, use it as a part of your negotiation strategy. (However, in the case of a relationship gone sour, I am not suggesting you find someone else first.)

Additionally, the authors of *Getting to Yes* stress that what makes you an even stronger negotiator is if you can reverse the table and determine what the other party's BATNA is. "Knowing their alternatives, you can realistically estimate what you can expect from the negotiation."

For example, if you are negotiating with a customer to close a deal and you know your customer's BATNA is going to another service provider, what can you do? You can prepare by researching all the other service providers and come up with an offer your customer cannot refuse.

After your preparation, you know your audience, you have a BATNA, and you know the other party's BATNA. What's next?

You have to listen. When you listen, you show respect to the other party and it helps with your negotiations.

A way to show you are a good listener is asking questions. Ask questions to show your true purpose is to seek understanding. That's right! Ask questions to listen. Ask questions to understand what the other party really means (don't just assume you understand). Questions make others feel good because you make an effort to see their point of view. Also, you may discover things that you never knew before.

When asking questions, consider the tone of your voice. Soften your questions so they come off as genuine. For example, instead of saying, "Why do you think that would work?" try to say, "I guess I am just wondering, how you think that would be the most successful approach?" The first question sends a message that you already know it won't work. The second makes an effort to understand the other party. You want to hear more before you jump to conclusions.

If you listen more than you talk, you are already succeeding in your negotiations.

Let's say your boss is unhappy with your performance. Whether your boss's perspective is justified or not, you must listen first. If you appear defensive and do all the talking, what will the result be? A conflict.

Another way to show you are a good listener is by paraphrasing or using the terminology of the other party. In other words, try to use similar vocabulary. For example, if the other party uses the term "car insurance" instead of your normally used term "vehicle insurance," use "car insurance" in your conversation. Using your own term signals that you are too focused on your own perspective, and you show disrespect.

In terms of paraphrasing, try to rephrase and repeat what the other party says from time to time. This sends a message that you listen and understand the other party's perspective. For example, you can say, "OK, I can see what you are trying to say." A shared trusting feeling thus develops.

Body language also plays a significant part. For example, when you sit or stand with the same posture, you show your willingness to listen. When you nod or keep your eyes focused, free from distraction, you show you are engaged. When you slightly relax your arms and hands on the table, you show you are open to hear the other person.

In addition, avoid furrowing your brow. Keep your gestures to a minimum as well. Always remain relaxed and calm, yet assertive. If you can listen with your body, you demonstrate that you are a very well-rounded listener.

Also, try to sit or stand, whatever circumstances apply, next to the other person. It appears that you are on the same team. In international soccer, when a referee discusses a call with a player or coach, the referee usually stands next to the other party, rather than face-to-face. It sends a message that they are on the same side, both committed to solving their differences. Try doing that as well when you are negotiating with others.

And when you are ready to conclude the negotiation and close the deal, make sure you consider the general atmosphere in the room before pushing for commitment.

Ask yourself a few questions: Is there a good feeling that both parties are satisfied with the arrangement so far? Does everyone involved feel they are heard and understood? Have mutual concerns been addressed? Are there small signals from the other party that they are comfortable to move forward?

And now you are ready for closure. Summarize the points you all agree on. Demonstrate you understand the other party's points of view and ensure they understand yours. From there, you can work towards setting up a plan of seeing an agreement through. And you can simply ask if the other party can agree to it and quietly wait for a response.

In the end, if you are struggling with negotiations, keep in mind a few things: first of all, you do it every day, have confidence! Remember those little times when you were successful with a negotiation. Second, be prepared— understand your audiences and have a BATNA. And finally, listen effectively.

Having effective negotiation skills is highly beneficial because it prepares you for another stressful aspect of work—team work. Everyone struggles with team work, but after taking the time to study the previous chapters, you should now be prepared to *know how teams operate.*

6

Know How Teams Operate

We all work in teams, regardless of our profession. Our family is our team. Our organization is our team. However, team work often presents challenges. In this chapter, we will analyze the different stages of team development.

In the 1960s, Bruce Tuckman, a professor of psychology, came up with the four stages of team development. These stages are: forming, storming, norming, and performing. Later, in the late 1970s, he added a fifth stage: adjourning. These stages act as an unavoidable cycle we constantly face, both in our professional lives and our personal lives. Basically, the stages are as follows.

Forming: This is when a new team is put together. Nervousness runs throughout the group. Group members find this moment exciting, but awkward. Excited in the sense that they are part of a new group. Awkward in the sense that roles and responsibilities are not defined clearly yet.

Storming: This is the stage which immediately follows forming. It is an inescapable stage characterized by jostling for positions and has potential for offending others. Group members are a bit reactive and defensive in this stage.

Norming: Once through the storming stage, the group settles into their established roles. In this stage, group members carry out their assigned duties, but may not feel like a true team yet. In other words, the group does not possess a shared purpose or team vision.

Performing: Although this stage is the ultimate goal, many teams may not reach this stage. In this stage, the group is in perfect sync and members work together for a shared purpose. They work together with passion, enthusiasm, and respect for each other. This is the "dream team" stage.

Adjourning: This final stage, which was added later, is there to help transition out of the performing stage. As the performing stage comes to an end, team members need to reflect on what made the team successful and recognize the skills contributed by their team members.

The fact of the matter is, we are constantly working through these stages. Look at a simple relationship for example:

A couple gets married and moves in together. There is apprehension and uncertainty, this is their forming stage. Then come the arguments about responsibilities, their storming stage. After routines are established, they get in their norming stage, both carrying out their tasks. Eventually, things really sync and their performing stage kicks in.

When a baby is coming, the couple needs that adjourning stage to reflect. This is when they celebrate their strengths that helped overcome their weaknesses. They are then prepared for the new forming stage.

When the baby arrives, the couple is back to their forming stage, there are mixed emotions. Storming follows, perhaps arguments about how often someone gets up to feed the baby, and so forth. Routine is established afterwards. And hopefully, everything comes together and they become a performing team again.

This cycle keeps playing out in their life. Every time a new event transpires in this family, a new cycle is born. It can be a new career move, an in-law moving in, or getting a new pet.

If personal relationships are that immersed in the cycles, you can only imagine how these stages play out in a work environment.

All teams pass through these stages. There is no skipping a stage. Of course we would all like to sneak from forming to performing, but that is impossible. In fact, when a new person, policy, factor, or event is brought in, a team automatically returns to the forming stage. And the cycle starts again.

You cannot avoid the stages, but you can decide how long you will be in them. You can also limit the severity of the forming and storming stages and move a team from the norming to performing stage with ease. It is up to you. Some teams never get out of the storming stage, while some linger in the norming stage, not reaching the "dream team" performing stage.

Now that you are aware of the unavoidable stages, let's talk about how you can move through them with relative ease.

Forming: If you know it is coming, you can prepare by setting up agreeable expectations. Make things transparent and open. Anticipate and be prepared for conflicts. For example, if you know a new team member is going to cause discomfort in the group, make an effort to ease the new person in. Discuss responsibilities so that everyone is clear about their roles. The group will feel less defensive immediately.

Storming: Some teams go through this in an hour, others a day, or even a year. If expectations and roles are made clear in the forming stage, you have something to fall back on. But the most important thing here is listening. Everyone has to listen or this stage can easily slip into chaos.

The bottom line is, we cannot ignore the storming stage, or hope it does not happen. We just have to anticipate it. When the forming stage is upon you, anticipate what the storming will be and try to minimize it. When the storming stage is upon you, be a listener, not a talker (use some of the listening skills you learned from the previous chapters). Let people vent their frustrations. This situation is challenging for everyone.

You cannot afford to be stuck in the storming stage, or you become a problem to your organization. Therefore, it is every team member's responsibility to help the group get out of this stage.

Norming: This stage is most characterized by team members carrying out no more than their assigned tasks. At this point, leadership is apparent and members' responsibilities are clear. But you are still just a group, not a team. You come to work, do your job and you go home. Ideally, you should want your team to achieve more. Unfortunately, this is the best many teams settle for.

This is a dangerous stage to settle in. If you are too comfortable in the norming stage, you risk being invisible.

When you are invisible, you are not "depended on," you are powerless. Hence, there must be an effort on everyone's behalf to move the team forward. Everyone must be committed. Encourage your team to come together.

Performing: This is the stage you want to be in. This is when your team syncs. Your organization sees that your team makes every effort to bring out the best in all involved. Your team is productive, your team is valuable, and your team is visible. Hence, you are productive, valuable, and visible.

In terms of understanding the difference between a norming team and a performing team, one only has to look at the Olympics. When high performance players are all put together on one national team, such is the case with hockey or soccer, there is a time when they are playing—just not as exceptionally as you would hope. That is because in the forming stage, one is chosen to be the captain among all of them. And since they may all be captains for their own professional teams, that leads to a bit of storming.

That's why taking all the best players from different teams to play in a team for the Olympics gold does not make the best team. It can be difficult for a very talented group to move from the forming stage to the performing stage in such a short period of time. And a lot of those teams really only make it to a norming stage. And we know for a fact, a gold medal is won by a performing team, not a norming team. A common cause, usually nationalistic pride, is what helps propel a team forward.

In other words, finding that common cause, and a shared purpose—that mutual commitment—is essential for achieving the performing stage. Your organization needs performing teams. You need performing teams. You need to be in performing teams. And you need to motivate yourself to want to be a performer not a "normer," and especially not a "stormer."

Adjourning: This recently added stage reminds us that when a project finishes or a team disbands, there needs to be a reflection process. This is when teams review their strengths and weaknesses, how they overcame challenges, and how they moved forward. Because once a new member joins the team, everything starts from the beginning again. And it is only by reflecting on what worked that you can prepare for the new forming and storming stages.

A SWOT (Strengths, Weaknesses, Opportunities, and Threats) analysis can be used in this adjourning stage to evaluate the team's performance during the previous stages. For example:

S: What are my or my team's strengths? What made my work or my team successful?

W: What are my or my team's weaknesses? What did not work for me or my team?

O: What opportunities do my or my team's project bring? What differences do I or my team bring to the organization?

T: What are the threats involved? Did I or my team stay in the storming or norming stage too long?

You can reflect on these questions alone or with your team. It is also helpful to reflect on these questions before joining a new team. You have to be aware of these stages. It is helpful to know what stage you are in with your colleagues, what impact you are having on your team or your colleagues, and what you can do to help your team or you and your colleagues to navigate through the storming stage.

By knowing how teams work, you increase your knowledge of the bigger picture, you put more into perspective. And to further help you get through the forming and storming stage, you need to know how to work with your team members or colleagues.

Another key factor in making teamwork effective is learning about the different personalities of the people around you have. So let's try to *understand personality styles*.

7

Understand Personality Styles

Several personality tests have emerged in recent years, all offering insights into yourself and others around you. Two frequently used tests are the Gregorc Style Delineator and the True Colors Test. Both offer exceptional tools and more or less come to the same conclusions about the different personality styles. What I would like to do here is summarize the findings of these tests into a simple-to-understand way. Identifying your personality is important, but more important is what to do with that information. You need to know your style and the style of others. This is so you can learn how to work effectively with the different styles, and most importantly, learn how to stretch your style to adapt to those different styles. Let's begin.

Style 1:
The planners, the schedulers, the organizers

Individuals in this category are organized and enjoy structure. They see things in a step-by-step progression. They favour routine and predictability, thus do not like surprises or unexpected changes. They fear uncertainty and instability.

They are very practical, extremely down-to-earth, and hands-on. They are very consistent and efficient with their work once they establish a routine.

They tend to believe actions speak louder than words, thus do not often give verbal compliments. Moreover, they care for details, but may be considered a bit picky over small things. Also, they believe in traditional family values and are extremely loyal to their organization.

Style 2:
The perfectionists, the researchers, the experts

Individuals in this category spend a lot of time—mostly alone—perfecting their skills. Their care for perfection may sometimes be mistaken for being competitive. However, competition is not what drives them.

They research and rely heavily on expert opinions, then apply their logic findings in their resolutions. They like intellectual stimulations, and may appear slightly aloof or disdainful to those of a "lesser" mind. They fear being disrespected or disregarded.

They are very quiet, and are often regarded as cold and distant. However, they are not the emotional type, they do not talk through their feelings with others.

Style 3:
The harmonizers, the humanizers, the empathizers

Individuals in this category are motivated by the need to connect emotionally with others. They like constant emotional reassurance. If they feel valued personally, they can move mountains. They are extremely friendly. They are strong listeners and they are concerned about people. As a result, they give as many compliments as they would like to receive.

They do not like conflicts; they want to be everyone's friend. Therefore, they would much rather sit on the fence than pick a side. They fear being rejected or unappreciated.

Additionally, they are flexible yet do not like restrictions. They focus on the big picture and can sometimes see beyond what is in front of them.

Style 4:
The innovators, the competitors, the risk-takers

Individuals in this category are driven to challenge the status quo with new or even untested ideas, by brainstorming innovative and exciting approaches. They take risks, pushing boundaries without fear of failure.

They are competitive by nature, and are driven to be recognized as the best among their peers. Even though they are optimistic and outgoing, they can get moody if they are not recognized for their special contributions.

Routine and doing the same things over and over is not for them. And they fear being controlled or restrained.

Different styles at work

Style 1

S1s like clear directions. They like to know what they are supposed to do and how to do it. If they are given instructions, they follow them through. They tend to be frustrated if they do not have a clear agenda or goal.

They like you to make a decision and see it through, without any sudden changes. Not being spontaneous, they may reject ideas that are suddenly raised or new methods that are presented without enough explanations.

They are strict yet fair. Rewards are given accordingly. However, they may get upset if everyone gets rewarded equally, especially if they think some of those individuals do not earn that reward.

Their care for details means they can keep very detailed reports. Small things, like being forgetful of the time, will bother them. Nevertheless, S1s work hard and lead by example. They bring order, stability, and loyalty to their work.

Style 2

S2s like to analyze situations before making a decision. They bring in research, facts, and statistics to support a logical proposition. Their desire for perfection makes them patient workers. They work hard at perfecting their work, gathering information and analyzing ideas.

They tend to get into business too promptly. They do not seem to make effort to build and foster interpersonal relationships. They may have researched and discovered the greatest solution to a problem, but the way they present their ideas can alienate others. Their colleagues may find them aloof and uncaring, and may reject their ideas because of the lack of emotional support prior to a meeting.

Therefore, diplomacy may be one of the biggest challenges for S2s. They have little room for sentimentality because they are very logical. And if they feel others' ideas are not well thought through, they may quickly dismiss those ideas. As a result, S2s simply do not like face-to-face meetings. Nevertheless, S2s work hard by constantly perfecting their skills. They bring logic, documentation, and their knowledge to their work.

Style 3

On the surface, they may appear to not take things so seriously and are even a bit unconcerned with specific details. However, S3s are extremely hard workers when they make personal connections with their managers. They need a boss to motivate them and make them feel good about themselves. And they thrive with constant praise.

On the other hand, they do not like to be confined by rules, thus they have a hard time with authority figures. They like flexibility. They like to be given complete trust and confidence in the work they do. Yet, they are good team players. They are good at providing support in times of need due to their highly empathetic nature.

Their ability to see the big picture also helps broaden the views of their colleagues, their teams, and their organization, although some may find they do not pay enough attention to detail. Nevertheless, S3s work hard by putting their hearts into their work. They bring harmony, empathy and their multi-dimensional vision to their work.

Style 4

S4s lead the way in innovation and design. Their fearless and multi-dimensional way of thinking pushes their work further ahead. However, they take risks. Their trial-and-error approach may seem too impulsive to their colleagues.

They like a career path that allows them to be who they are and allows their talents to blossom. They need an atmosphere of freedom to be creative and expressive. Also, they like to work independently; hence, they are not entirely team players. However, for competition's sake, they do their part to try and make a team work.

Yet, other styles may find it difficult working with them because they have issues with individuals who follow rules too closely as well as with authority figures who make the rules. On top of that, they can get easily bored and become overly playful at work. Nevertheless, S4s work hard by brainstorming new ideas. They bring innovations, stimulations, and their multi-dimensional visions to their work.

Style stretching summary:

So we have analyzed the different personality styles, now it's time to learn how we can stretch ourselves to adapt to the different styles.

Style 1

- Try to be less defensive when change is discussed (be more flexible)

- Try to understand that others do not see routines as important as you do (some other styles are not motivated by routines)

- Try to give more compliments to the other styles (some other styles need compliments)

- Try not to get frustrated over small things (step back and look at the bigger picture)

- Try to think more outside the box (be more accepting of different perspectives)

Style 2

- Try to focus less on perfection with your expectations of others (learn to settle for less sometimes)

- Try to make time for building personal relationships (before presenting an idea, make a little time to break the ice and have a little small talk)

- Try to listen better (work on hearing people out even if their perspectives are not research based)

- Try to be less serious with conversations (not every conversation needs to be an intellectual discussion)

- Try to explore more on the emotional side of aspects (some other styles need emotional connections and support)

Style 3

- Try to expect less emotional investment from others (some other styles are not as emotionally in tune)

- Try to be less relaxed (show more concern for details)

- Try to keep your emotions and feelings to yourself (if you open yourself up too much, you may get hurt)

- Try to be more firm with opinions (pick a side)

- Try to be less demanding for compliments (some other styles are not good at giving compliments)

Style 4

- Try to remember that not everything is a competition (some other styles are not competitive)

- Try to be more serious at work (be less distracted when others are talking to you)

- Try to understand that people who follow rules are conscientious and loyal (be more respectful to others)

- Try to slow down, be a little more sedate at work (some other styles are very serious)

- Try to be a better team player (include others in your work, share your ideas)

You may be able to add more to the lists, especially since now you have a better understanding of the different styles.

The fact is, although some people fit neatly into one specific style, we are often a blend of these styles. Like every style, we see the world though our own eyes and we often make the wrong assumption that everyone sees the world as we do. The reality is the styles that least characterize us probably present the biggest challenges for us. And if you look back over your life, you may find that those are the styles that created stress for you.

So what can we do? We should not attempt to change others or change ourselves to match them. Instead, we should try to understand our style, anticipate others' styles, and learn to live with each other's differences. Lastly and most importantly, we need to try to stretch our style.

After learning about the different personality styles, you should function better with others already. However, there are more differences, other than personalities, at work these days. Let's explore more. Let's learn to be open and *accept generational differences*!

8

Accept Generational Differences

Something very interesting occurred in a communication course I taught recently. During the introductions, a student introduced herself by saying she just started college and then said, "And I'm nineteen." People do not usually mention their age with their introduction, but she felt it was important to. The next morning, I woke up with the significant realization that she is nineteen, the oldest of Generation Z. Wow! Generation Z has started college!

Generation Z is starting that first step in studying the world's problems in more depth. The baton is now passed to them. They are tasked with solving the problems we left behind. I wonder what solutions they will bring, what kind of citizens they will become. As the world still grapples with Generation Y, everyone is now faced with a new challenge.

Understanding how different generations process information is essential. Because today, you can be working with five different generations, each born from different socio-economic and technological times. And ultimately, we all have a responsibility to adapt to one another. By analyzing the different generations, you are better prepared to work with them. You show that you are a valuable asset for your organization.

I summarized the findings of different generations and am presenting them in different categories. By learning about each generation's background (social, economic, family, technology), we can have a better understanding of their characters and their work attitudes. So let's begin!

Generally, the five generations are as follows:

The Traditional Generation Also known as Veterans, the Silent Generation, and the Greatest Generation	Born between 1922 and 1946
The Baby Boomer Generation	Born between 1946 and 1965
Generation X Also known as the Lost Generation	Born between 1965 and 1980
Generation Y Also known as the Echo Boomers, Millennial Generation, and Generation Next	Born between 1980 and 1995
Generation Z Also known as the Digital Generation, iGeneration, and Net Generation	Born after 1995 and who are now 20 and under

The years are meant to be general guidelines of when each generation begins. There are also types of generational hybrids whose lifespans overlap the generational divides. But to keep this general and simple, we are not discussing them here.

Some general characteristics:

- Traditionalists are regarded as traditional, loyal, and disciplined, yet are submissive to authority and tech-challenged.

- Baby boomers are regarded as optimistic, hard-working, and goal-oriented, yet are competitive and narcissistic.

- Generation Xers are regarded as independent, pragmatic, and individualistic, yet are skeptical and pessimistic.

- Generation Yers are regarded as confident, sophisticated, and open-minded, yet are attention-craving and feel entitled.

- Generation Zers are regarded as entrepreneurial, prudent, and unbiased, yet are impatient and lack personal skills.

Brief background (social and economic):

Traditionalists were raised during the Great Depression, times of plagues, and wars. This generation is small and hence enjoyed more opportunities due to a lack of competition.

The Baby Boomers were raised in a time of economic prosperity due to the end of the Second World War. There was a significant increase in birth rate as a result. Competitions were fierce due to the big population, thus many of them moved to the cities for education and career opportunities.

Generation X grew up in a time of economic uncertainty. This generation witnessed the dark side of institutional ethics and was threatened with nuclear war. As a result, they were told that they may not enjoy the advantages that previous generations had.

Generation Y has the largest population since the Baby Boomers, hence competition was more severe. However, this generation generally grew up in an era of optimism, that is, up until the shocking tragedy of 9/11.

Generation Z is also emerging as a big group with a global population of two billion. The oldest of this generation were 6 years old when 9/11 happened. Research indicates that this generation is facing a complex world full of uncertainty and turmoil. But due to the economic times, they generally have the best the world can offer, and they are quite optimistic going forward.

Family background:

Traditionalists were raised in traditional homes. In most cases, fathers were breadwinners and mothers were homemakers.

Divorces became fairly common for the Baby Boomers. They started to question and even reject traditional values at times.

Gen X spent very little time with their parents. With both parents working, Gen X became independent problem-solvers. However, being aware of the amount of broken homes, they approached relationships cautiously.

According to the US Census Bureau, in 2008, about 75% of Gen Yers were growing up in a two-parent household in which they received a high level of support (both emotionally and financially) from their parents.

Only two-thirds (about 67%) of Gen Z live with both parents. Also, according to current census data, about 250 000 children of this generation in the United States are being raised by same-sex couples. And with mixed marriages being more common, researchers suggest that this generation is so far the most diverse and inclusive.

Technology:

Traditionalists are often seen as resistant to today's technology. But despite being "tech-challenged," Traditionalists were technological forerunners in their own way. They introduced TV to the world and made groundbreaking discoveries issued in the space age.

For the Baby Boomers, technology was a status symbol. The possession of up-to-date devices represented financial superiority. And with their pursuit of technological advancements, space travel and the Internet were made possible.

For Gen X, technology was a practical part of life. Computers became fairly accessible at home, at school, and at work. They see technology as a way to reach people faster and easier.

Gen Y had even more technology in their life as the Internet took root in the early 1990s. For them, computers, tablets, and the Internet are essential work tools. Emails, text messaging, and webinars are their common means of communication.

Unlike any previous generations, Generation Z is truly defined by technology. They are considered "the first tribe of true digital natives" or "screenagers." Being born "wired from the crib," they've never known a time without interactive technology. To them, technology represents instant worldwide communication and information access.

Work (environment/attitudes):

Traditionalists come from a very different work culture, a workplace dominated by men. Moreover, Traditionalists are very loyal employees who are unlikely to change jobs for career advancement. They generally follow a top-down chain of command and avoid conflict at work. The one critique of this generation seems to be their being slow to change.

Baby Boomers also like a hierarchal or rank-based system. They may find it hard to work in a flexible environment. But unlike the Traditionalists, Boomers are unafraid of confrontations; they may even challenge the status quo. However, they take their careers very seriously. They were the first to introduce using personality tests at work to help colleagues get along.

For Gen X, work is just a job. This generation values a work-life balance. They are the "work hard, play hard" generation who like to incorporate fun activities at work. However, members of this generation are generally not devoted to a single employer, perhaps due to witnessing their parents' struggle to keep their jobs during tough economic times. Gen X places a high value on education, and many become professionals as a result.

Gen Y looks for fulfillment at work. They want to be appreciated as good employees, and they want encouraging managers. However, after generally being pampered through life, they like to be coached and mentored along the way. Hence, the reputation that they act entitled. Like Gen Xers, Gen Yers are very educated. And with an education system of "no child left behind," Gen Yers are generally very motivated in their education, resulting in a saturation of professionals among this generation.

In the article, "Meet Generation Z: Forget everything you learned about Millennials," Gen Zers are generally regarded as entrepreneurial. Overall 60% of them look for work that makes a social difference and 72% want to start their own business to achieve this. However, they do not place as high value in becoming professionals, such as doctors and scientists. As a result, we may have a shortage of professionals when Gen Z dominate the workplace.

What does it all mean?

We can learn something valuable from each generation. And we can apply our understanding of their different values to work better with each other.

Traditionalists exemplify the spirit of loyalty, hard work and determination. Their being steady and down-to-earth also allows them to put work in perspective and not create conflict. However, traditionalists need to keep up with today's technology and work pace. Organizations can provide training courses to help improve their technological skills. And when introducing new ideas, keep in mind that this group is slow to change and allow them more time to adapt.

Baby Boomers encourage us to question ineffective status quos. They teach us that conflict can be constructive and respectful. However, Baby Boomers need to be careful of how they approach conflict. Effective communication skills are thus essential for them and for those working with them.

Gen X teaches us that humour is sometimes beneficial in the workplace. However, their approach to work has to change in order to survive in today's workplace. They have to put more effort into their work or they risk being invisible and not depended on. When working with Gen Xers, try to find different approaches to motivate and encourage them.

Gen Yers make us question the value of our work. They want their work to be meaningful. Managers can motivate this group by giving more encouragement. However, Gen Y needs to be more independent in solving problems. Demanding too much handholding can make them a problem for their managers or their organizations.

Gen Zers truly define diversity and inclusion. We all have to learn from this generation to be more accepting. However, Gen Zers need to be more patient for those who are not so spontaneous. Remember that not everyone grew up with instant technology. Nevertheless, the rest of us have to keep up, or risk falling behind.

Conclusion:

By learning different generations' perspectives, we can forge stronger relationships at work. We can learn from different generations' strengths and help tackle their weaknesses. Remember we are all part of the team. And we all have responsibilities to get our team to the performing stage.

We cannot change people, but we can adapt to them. If you cannot stretch yourself to adapt, you outlive your usefulness to the organization. The workplace is very diverse; you therefore need to be open-minded, flexible, and adaptable. And with your empathy quotient higher, and your compassion for others' perspective more developed, you are now ready to *embrace diversity and inclusion.*

9

Embrace Diversity and Inclusion

Companies often require their employees to take a diversity course. Why? It is important to analyze your openness to diversity and inclusion.

Many people think they are open to diversity, but they are not. In September 2008, an Indigenous man, Brian Sinclair, died in a Winnipeg emergency room after waiting for 34 hours. He died when his catheter got blocked and caused an infection in his bladder. It was simple to treat, but the staff just thought he was a drunk sleeping off a hangover there. So he died in that waiting area without treatment.

This sad occurrence is just one of millions of our daily global tragedies. Why wasn't Brian treated immediately? Why did the staff assume he was drunk? Was it because he was an Indigenous person? Was it because the staff were not open to diversity? Where was their sense of morality?

In fact, our view of diversity and inclusion is closely related to our stage of moral development. If you want to be an adaptable and respectable team player, take time to review your stage of moral development.

American psychologist, Lawrence Kohlberg concluded that a person graduates through various stages of moral development. There are six stages, divided over three categories: pre-conventional, conventional, and post-conventional. By understanding which stage you are in, you are better able to see how you need to grow and stretch yourself.

Pre-conventional:

In the first stage, individuals' decisions are driven by a fear of punishment. For example, a person will not cheat on a test for fear of being punished, not for any significant moral reasoning. At this stage, moral reasoning is unclear.

By stage two, individuals recognize different perspectives; however, decisions are driven by their own desires. In many cases, individuals act for their own benefit. For example, if a child is given a snack for cleaning his room, he would actually clean his room for the snack. At this stage, individuals may even break rules without feeling guilty if they are not caught.

Conventional:

In stage three, individuals discover that good behaviour is rewarded and they are adored as a result. However, their decisions are driven by group pressure. They tend to follow the larger group consensus because they want approval from their peers. The closest they may come to standing up for a principle would be defending a person who has fallen out of favour, "He tried…I am sure he didn't mean any harm…" But if the larger group asserts pressure, they may recoil and simply agree with the larger group's assessment.

In stage 4, individuals begin to adopt a sense of right and wrong. They develop a very black and white perspective of morality; however, it is still very much based on outside perspectives. They stick to values of their upbringings and the law as it stands. For them, the law is absolute. If one person is allowed to get away with something, everyone will try to get away with it, which leads to chaos.

Individuals in this conventional category can be stubborn, unwavering, and unable to separate their reasoning from their upbringing's preprogramming. These individuals might make decisions based on answers to the question "What would my parents do in this situation?" They live with influential ghosts in their heads. We just have to hope those ghosts are reasonable ones.

Post-conventional:

In stage 5, individuals notice that different laws and expectations apply to different cultures and communities. They are aware of exceptions to rules. In other words, at this stage, individuals question the validity of laws, or even the principles of their upbringing. These individuals are more tolerant of diversity and can interact more easily with different types of people. They are adaptable and open-minded.

And the point worth making here is, according to Kohlberg, many people do not cross over from stage 4 to stage 5. This is the hardest gap to cross. It takes a major shift to take that step. Those in stage 4 are afraid to step away from their black and white world because they are so influenced by their upbringing and personal beliefs. They are so grounded in those values that they miss opportunities to challenge those beliefs.

This brings us to the final stage. Kohlberg indicated that very few cases actually apply in this stage. Stage 6, the most empathetic stage, is the one in which individuals see a situation entirely from other people's perspectives and try to understand their values and beliefs. They consider all aspects of the others' perspectives, including the policies and laws that dictate their actions and their background and beliefs, and they arrive at a decision based on seeing the reality though other people's eyes. I suppose the closest comparison is found in films like *Dances with Wolves* or *Avatar*, in which the person takes the initiative to abandon all that they know and live a life completely according to another culture and realize that they need to question their own morals.

In the end, for most of us, achieving a stage 5 level of moral development is challenging enough; but actually transforming ourselves into another person in level 6 takes a great deal of courage.

Nevertheless, not all circumstances require us to function at a stage 6. At stage 6, as indicated in the cases of *Dances with Wolves* and *Avatar*, the characters choose to follow their own convictions, caring nothing for the opinions of others, fearing neither imprisonment nor death. How many of us are willing to make such a sacrifice for an empathetic cause? In fact, how many people do we know who consistently function at this stage?

In most circumstances, one can be well-rounded, level-headed, open-minded, and generally empathetic in stage 5. In the workplace, stage 5 is where we want to operate. Therefore, before making any decisions, you first need to ask yourself: *Am I letting personal biases and preconceived ideas overshadow my decisions?*

In the end, the key to being a productive and respectful individual is being concerned about and empathetic to others. Apply everything you learn from the previous chapters, and truly open your mind to accept those who are different from yourself. Let's push ourselves past stage 4; let's put ourselves in other people's shoes to make a well-balanced, open-minded, and compassionate contribution to our workplace.

We live in a world that demands us to put ourselves in other people's shoes. Now more than ever, in this global village, how you view and interact with others—different from yourself—determines your value in your organization.

By learning to put diversity and inclusion in perspective, you increase your emotional intelligence. You must open your mind and be more accepting of others. You need to self-reflect and be open to alternative solutions. You need to put things in perspective. And that may involve making an effort to evolve your moral development or even questioning your existing values.

We all need to identify our moral development stage because only once we reach that stage 5 can empathy begin to take root. What is holding you back? Is your perspective black and white? Are you afraid to have opinions different from those who raised or taught you? Can you make your own assertions about the world? Do you see that grey areas sometimes need to exist? Sometimes it is in those grey areas that respect for humanity resides.

Fortunately, respect for diversity and inclusion is increasing. However, it is still quite slow or non-existent in various communities. The challenge here is to continue and dig deeper. The more we learn about people's values and beliefs, the stronger we can develop relationships.

So after all is said and done, this brings us to the most important point: many organizations are having a difficult time keeping ahead of the curve and keeping up with current trends. Now more than ever, organizations are shaking their own organizational tree looking for employees to offer innovative ideas that help move the organization forward. You need to be the one contributing those ideas and solutions to your organization—this is the new power! This is what today's organizations ultimately depend on you for. And you can only be in a position to offer solutions if you routinely apply all the skills from the previous chapters. The next step for you is into a leadership position. And to get ready for this position, you have to *start thinking like a leader*.

10

Start Thinking Like a Leader

As the world of work continues to be reshaped by economic forces, many organizations are looking inward to fill their leadership ranks. However, this proves to be a difficult task time and time again. Taking your best employees and turning them into managers does not mean they will be the best managers. But the pressure is on.

Recently, more and more organizations are approaching corporate training entities to provide leadership skills training at an earlier stage so their staff are more prepared to lead when the time comes. What we want to examine here is what that early preparation looks like. How can you develop those leadership skills now?

These days, we are inundated with theories about what makes a great leader great. Many see leaders as individuals who inspire others to follow their vision. However, most organizations are not exactly looking for the next Martin Luther King, Jr.; instead, the majority of those asked to step up to a leadership role are simply individuals who have passion for their work. Because their passion gets results, management wants them to transfer that passion to their colleagues, which would benefit the organization as a whole.

So if you want to be visible, if you want to be depended on, and if you want your organization to see that you possess leadership qualities, you need to have passion for what you do. And it is not enough to tell people you have passion, you need to ooze it. You need to put 110% effort into your work.

Now you may be thinking, *I am passionate and I do love what I do, but no one notices. And I watch people all around me getting those promotions I feel I have also worked hard for.... What am I missing?*

Well, it is time to look in the mirror and really make an effort to see how others are actually perceiving you.

In his book *Good Boss, Bad Boss: How to Be the Best...and Learn from the Worst*, Robert Sutton uncovers that the best leaders are actually "self-obsessed"—in a good way. They are constantly asking themselves how others perceive them. Sutton emphasizes that leaders are under an intense light.

In many ways, your colleagues know more about you than you think they do. They are always watching you. When they get your emails, they are reading between the lines. When you come to work, they are assessing your mood or demeanour for any tell-tale signs that something is not well.

So how are you actually perceived by others? The following is a checklist to help you "look in the mirror":

- Am I visible? (Do people know I exist? Or do I just come to work, do my job and leave when the day ends?)

- How do I look? (Do I dress according to the accepted norms of my organization, work group, or professional station at work?)

- How is my body language perceived? (Do I mirror the body language of others in conversations to show interest in what they say?)

- Do I listen more than I talk? (Or am I a *conversational narcissist*?)

- Do I help others as much as they help me? (Do I have a balanced work relationship with others? If they are doing more for me than I do for them, they may start to resent me.)

- Am I positive about the organization? (Do I find myself complaining about the management?)

- Do I volunteer? (Do I make myself cheerfully available for work-related functions or extra shifts?)

- Are my emails polite? (Do I understand that an email is the same as a conversation? In other words, my email should be in the same wording and tone as if I were to stand next to the receiver and read it to them.)

- Am I accepting of others and their needs? (Am I known for being open-minded about different personalities, generations, diversity, and inclusion?)

- Do I actively encourage and motivate people? (Am I supportive and kind to my colleagues? Could they imagine me as their leader? Or am I unapproachable, close-minded, snobby, stubborn, aloof, and cold?)

- Do I say negative things about others? (Am I a character assassin? Do I like to bring others down so I look better than I do?)

- Do I know my role in a team? (Am I a supportive team member? Do I help my team to reach the performing stage? Or do I hoard information, steal ideas, put others down, and create conflict?)

In short, this checklist helps to determine if you are "other focused."

You may be familiar with some of these questions, especially if you read my first book. And you can add some of your own questions to the checklist. Nonetheless, these questions all interact together to show your passion at work. You need to know how you are perceived. You need to have a good reputation (If your reputation is not good, you need to work on that). You need to bring in that 110% effort. Extend your contributions from just doing your required work to helping others at work too. Provide your premium customer service. Apply all you learn to be a good listener and an empathetic individual. Now, that's passion!

Not only that, you need to be the one who is always on the lookout for new ideas and approaches. And before proposing your ideas, it is helpful to first understand how to present them. If your idea is to be successful, you need to first get buy in from close supporters who are open-minded and appreciative of new ideas. Then have them help you sell your ideas.

If you start by lobbying for support for your ideas, your ideas gain ground. Many people are afraid to share their ideas for fear that someone might steal them. But when they drop the idea at a general meeting, the idea doesn't get supported. Because by holding back that idea in the first place and only bringing it up at the meeting, it looks like you hoarded the idea selfishly to make yourself look better than your team. And like many new ideas, there will be resistance, and who do you have to support you then?

So your idea dies. You lose credibility. Management sees you cannot motivate or lead others, or worse, you hoard good ideas and suddenly present them in a general meeting for your own selfish gains. And it is clear to everyone around the table what leadership means to you— it's all about *you*.

Leadership is not about you. It's not about how great *you* are. It's how you can actually lead and motivate others around you. If you want to be a leader, you have to show people that you have what it is to lead. Don't be afraid to share your ideas. It makes others feel more confident in you.

This is what you need to do. First, build a network and apply skills from previous chapters to do this. Get buy in for your ideas before you present them. In this way, you are empowering others, not just showing how great your ideas are. (Always remember Edison's' lesson: Respect people in the process.) You cannot be the next leader in your team, department, or organization without the support of your colleagues. So develop those relationships.

As a result, your colleagues will help you get your idea through to the large majority. And in the process, you have shared your idea and involved others (their success is your success). So identify those who will support you, surround yourself with them, empower them with your ideas, and let them empower you as well. If you plan well, and build solid relationships with those you work with, your goal of becoming a leader is already achieved.

In 1869, before the new territory of Manitoba became a province, one of the Canadian fathers of confederation, Louis Riel, had a vision. He saw that Canada's government needed to be more just, open, and fair with its citizens. He gathered like-minded individuals and convinced them of his idea. Together, they then went out to the various communities throughout the territory to spread that idea, until a general acceptance was achieved. And before Louis Riel drafted the *Manitoba Act* (which made Manitoba the fifth official province of Canada on July 15, 1870), he made sure he approached every community in that territory to learn about what they wanted. As a result, the *Manitoba Act* remains one of the most beautifully and humanly drafted documents in history. It takes into account the civil rights of all the different Indigenous groups, French and English settlers, and all Catholics and Christians alike.   Every walk of life, in Manitoba at that time, had a say in the making of this new province, and everyone's rights were protected. Everyone owned it. It wasn't just Louis Riel's province, it was theirs as well. Support for his leadership therefore expanded.

So, the lesson here is: discover new ideas, surround yourself with supporters (and they support you because you support them), then inspire them to own the ideas—while respecting their ideas as well—and they will help you convince the majority to accept your ideas and let this process elevate you to that next role.

Apart from being self-reflective and better with communicating your innovative ideas, one final piece must be in place for you to be recognized as an individual with leadership potential: you must understand your organization's vision, mission, goals, and values and apply all of that to everything you do.

For example, if your organization's values are collaboration and fairness, you have to ask yourself: *Do I collaborate with my colleagues, other departments, and stakeholders? Do I treat people fairly and equally? Do I give people opportunities to improve and better themselves?*

Take your time to review your organization's values and try to live them through your work. Make the vision of your organization your vision. By knowing your organization's vision, you can also help colleagues see values in their positions. The story below illustrates the importance of this point.

A few years ago, I taught a course on leadership to a group of janitors for the local school board. On the wall of the training room was the school board's vision statement: "Educating Tomorrow's Citizens Today." This statement is printed on every school document. This statement is on the walls of every lunch room and every department, from the boiler room in the school at the farthest outskirts of the city to the executive offices downtown. I asked the janitors if this statement added any meaning to their work. Many confessed that they had worked there so long they forgot the statement was even there. Others said that's only there for teachers and people who work directly with children. Some remarked that if they really thought about it, they could find some kind of a connection.

Suddenly a course participant, who had been very quiet throughout the course, spoke up. She had been working for the school board for many years and this discussion brought back a memory for her.

She said that when she first became a janitor, she hated the job. She explained that all she did was clean up vomit and crap all day. She said when she cleaned a room and saw that vision she would smirk sarcastically and mutter, "More like cleaning up the crap of tomorrow's citizens today."

But one day that all changed. During a lunch break, a colleague came in and joined her. Noticing that she wasn't very happy, he asked her what that vision meant to her. She responded negatively, explaining that she was just a lowly janitor with nothing to contribute but cleaning skills.

"Then that colleague said something to me that changed my life. And I would never forget." she said.

He asked her what the word "janitor" meant. He said it came from ancient times and it was originally based on the word for "doorkeeper" and he said that's what she was.

"You open those doors every day. You watch out for the kids. You shovel the snow and salt the steps. You provide a safe and clean environment for these young children."

He told her she did just as much or even more than any employee of that school board in helping educate tomorrow's citizens, by providing the best possible educational environment.

And from that day forward, she became a doorkeeper. She kept a watchful eye out for the students, and did everything in her power to make sure she did her part to always create a safe and clean learning environment. She grew to love her job more than anything. She is indebted to that colleague who helped her see her part in the school board's vision. Not only did it give meaning to her job but to her life as well. And now she is helping her fellow colleagues see their parts.

Do you see what that janitor's colleague brought to his organization? He was a true leader. He recognized that all leaders have a responsibility to help others see meaning in their work. A true leader knows how to apply—and help others apply—the vision, mission, and values of an organization in their work.

So, know your organization's vison, mission, and values, and live them. Encourage others to align their efforts and goals with them as well.

In the end, if you want to be promoted to a leadership positon, these three points will help you attain that goal. First, you need to be incredibly self-obsessed, so you know how you stand in your organization. Second, apply all you learn to build your network of support for your ideas (and make sure you help others as much as they help you). And finally, know and live your organization's values, and use that to motivate your colleagues as well.

Be the passionate, empathetic leader everyone wants to follow!

Conclusion

The world of work is constantly shifting and changing. We have no choice but to shift and change with it. With globalization, environmental issues, and the pursuit of a more open perspective on diversity and inclusion, we are tasked with bringing a much more diverse communication skill set to the table. We need to open our minds to wider opportunities and awareness. We have to stay abreast of the latest technological advancements and the fast-paced dynamics of change management, and we have to respect others throughout the process.

However, you don't want to be in a position of just keeping up. If you work hard to apply the simple tactics this book proposes, you will in fact find yourself ahead of the curve and be able to anticipate what the future brings. All you need to do is stop and take a look at the big picture. Put everything into perspective. Take a look in the mirror and ask yourself:

1. *Do I provide supreme customer service (to both my external and internal customers)?*
2. *Do I treat others the way I wish to be treated?*
3. *Am I visible and depended on at your work?*
4. *Am I networking in an effective way?*
5. *Am I current and up-to-date at my work?*
6. *Do I listen, or do I do most of the talking?*
7. *Are my conversations more about me or others?*
8. *Am I skilled at difficult conversations?*
9. *Am I confident in my negotiations?*
10. *Am I a good team player?*

11. *Am I able to make my own moral opinions about the world?*
12. *Am I flexible and open to change?*
13. *Do I stretch my personality style for others?*
14. *Am I adaptable to different generations?*
15. *Do I embrace diversity and inclusion?*
16. *Do I have passion for my work?*
17. *Do I bring in and share new and innovative ideas for my work?*
18. *Do I know and live my organization's vision?*
19. *Do I feel, think, and act like a leader?*
20. *Would I hire me?*

After reflecting on these questions, you see the bigger picture of your world. Then it is time to think about your next move —where do you see yourself in five years.

"Where do you see yourself in five years?" is a frequently asked question in interviews, regardless of the profession. It is a question designed for the interviewer to measure if you think beyond the interview. It is designed to see if you have reflected on your strengths and weaknesses. It is designed to see if you have made efforts to overcome your weaknesses while enhancing your strengths.

It is a valid question and should not simply be considered for preparation for another interview. It is one you should seriously consider on your own.

It is important to make that five-year plan, so you can give focus to your career path. If you want to be a regional manager in five years, what do you need to do right now to attain that goal? If you want to be a leader in another company in five years, what do you do to make that a reality? Five-year plans give you the focus you need.

Additionally, you can start to create several attainable short-term goals for yourself. After making a plan and mapping out where you want to be in five years, start taking the right steps. Little by little, analyze your interactions with people. Embrace feedback, especially negative feedback. And act accordingly with the information. Use it to make changes in your behaviour or in the way you deal with others. We can't change overnight, but we can take steps to put us where we need to be. Ask yourself: *Where do I want to be in five years?* Then ask: *What do I need to do to prepare myself for it?*

In the end, you are in control of your own destiny. Start now! Apply the 10 tips in this book to take that significant first step. Take into account all you learn from this book and start thinking and acting like a leader. On the other hand, if you already incorporate these tips in your life and are achieving success, congratulations! Nevertheless, pass this information along to others, so they too may encounter your success.

References

Beebe, S. A., Beebe, S. J., Redmond, M. V., & Geerinck, T. M. (2015). *Interpersonal Communication: Relating to Others* (6th ed.). Toronto, ON: Pearson Canada Inc.

Boyden, Joseph (2010). *Louis Riel and Gabriel Dumont.* Toronto, ON: Penguin Group.

Drucker, P. F. (2008). *Managing Oneself.* Boston, MA: Harvard Business Press.

Fisher, R., Ury, W. L., Patton, B. (2011). *Getting to Yes: Negotiating Agreement Without Giving In.* New York, NY: Penguin Books Ltd.

Frank N. Magid Associates, Inc. (2014). *The First Generation of the Twenty-First Century: An introduction to The Pluralist Generation.* Retrieved from http://magid.com/sites/default/files/pdf/MagidPluralist GenerationWhitepaper.pdf

Gregorc, Anthony, F. (2009). *Gregorc Style Delineator™: A Self-assessment Instrument for Adults.* Columbia, CT: Gregorc Associates, Inc.

Irving, K. (Producer), Christensen, D. (Producer), & Wolochatiuk, T. (Director). (2012). *We Were Children* [Motion Picture Documentary]. Canada: National Film Board of Canada.

Jung, C. G., & Franz, M.-L. v. (1964). *Man and his Symbols.* Garden City, NY: Doubleday.

Kane, S. (2015). *The Multigenerational Workforce: Managing and Motivating Multiple Generations in the Legal Workplace.* Retrieved from http://legalcareers.about.com/od/practicetips/a/multige neration.htm

Kingston, A. (2014). *Get ready for Generation Z.* Retrieved from http://www.macleans.ca/society/life/get-ready-for-generation-z/

Kohlberg, L. (1984). *The Psychology of Moral Development: The Nature and Validity of Moral Stages (Essays on Moral Development, Volume 2).* New York, USA: Harper & Row

Landau, J. (Producer), & Cameron, J. (Director). (2009). *Avatar* [Motion picture]. USA: 20th Century Fox.

Langton, N., Robbins, S. P., & Judge, T., A. (2013). *Fundamentals of Organizational Behaviour, Fifth Canadian Edition.* Toronto, ON: Pearson Education Inc.

Maslow, A. H. (1943). A theory of human motivation. *Psychological Review, 50,* 370–396.

Miscisin, M. (2001). *Showing Our True Colors.* Riverside, CA: True Colors.

Mojtehedzadeh, S., & Monsebraaten, L. (2015). Precarious work is now the new norm, United Way report says. *Toronto Star.* Retrieved from http://www.thestar.com/news/gta/2015/05/21/precario us-work-is-now-the-new-norm-united-way-report-says.html

Newton, J. (1989). *Uncommon Friends: Life with Thomas Edison, Henry Ford, Harvey Firestone, Alexis Carrel, and Charles Lindbergh.* San Diego, CA: Harvest/HBJ.

Palmer, A. (2014). Are you X, Y, Z, Boomer or Silent Generation – What Does it Mean for You? *Mirror.* Retrieved from http://www.mirror.co.uk/news/uk-news/you-x-y-z-boomer-3950868

Pearlman, J. (2015). Australian mother attacked by Facebook friends over constant baby posts. *The Telegraph.* Retrieved from http://www.telegraph.co.uk/technology/facebook/11537313/Australian-mother-attacked-by-Facebook-friends-over-constant-baby-posts.html

Puxley, C. (2014). Brian Sinclair inquest told aboriginals face racism in ERs. *The Canadian Press.* Retrieved from http://www.cbc.ca/news/canada/manitoba/brian-sinclair-inquest-told-aboriginals-face-racism-in-ers-1.2670990

Schroer, W. J. (2013). Generations X, Y, Z and the Others. *The Social Librarian.* Retrieved from http://www.socialmarketing.org/newsletter/features/generation1.htm

Seidman, G. (2014). Is Facebook Really Turning Us into Narcissists?: Facebook use may be a consequence, and not a cause, of narcissism. *Psychology Today.* Retrieved from https://www.psychologytoday.com/blog/close-encounters/201408/is-facebook-really-turning-us-narcissists

Sparks & Honey. (2014). Meet Generation Z: Forget everything you learned about Millennials. *SlideShare*. Retrieved from http://www.slideshare.net/sparksandhoney/generation-z-final-june-17

Stout, M. (2005). *The Sociopath Next Door*. New York, NY: Broadway Books.

Sutton, R. I. (2010). *Good Boss, Bad Boss: How to Be the Best ... and Learn from the Worst*. New York, NY: Business Plus.

Tirado, Bernardo (2011). Generations + Technology – How the Web Is Being Used by Generations. *Psychology Today*. Retrieved from https://www.psychologytoday.com/blog/digital-leaders/201111/generations-technology

Truth and Reconciliation Commission of Canada. (2015). *Honouring the Truth, Reconciling for the Future: Final Report of the Truth and Reconciliation Commission of Canada*. Retrieved from http://www.trc.ca/websites/trcinstitution/File/2015/Findings/

Tuckman, B. W., & Jensen, M. A. C. (2010). Stages of small-group development revisited. *Group Facilitation*, 10, 43–48. Retrieved from http://search.proquest.com/docview/747969212?accountid=13652

Wilson, J. (Producer), & Costner, K. (Director). (1990). *Dances with Wolves* [Motion picture]. USA: Orion Pictures.

Wilson, T. (2013). Reference letters can invite lawsuits from former employees. *The Globe and Mail.* Retrieved from http://www.theglobeandmail.com/report-on-business/small-business/sb-managing/human-resources/reference-letters-can-invite-lawsuits-from-former-employees/article14726527/

Index

About the Author

Matt Adolphe, author of *Canadian Workplace Culture: Mastering the Unspoken Rules*, has an extensive background facilitating courses and seminars focusing on workplace communication. Currently, he is an instructor at the Southern Alberta Institute of Technology, and a private consultant. He is well regarded for his passion in helping individuals find success in their careers. He holds a Master's Degree in Communication Management, and lives in Calgary, Alberta.

CPSIA information can be obtained at www.ICGtesting.com
Printed in the USA
LVOW10s0601040216

473585LV00001B/7/P